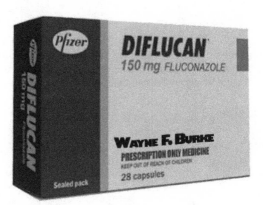

BareBackPress

This is a work of fiction. The characters, incidents, and dialogue are the products of the author's imagination and are not to be construed as real. Any resemblance to actual events or person, living or dead, is entirely coincidental.

BareBackPress
Hamilton, Ontario, Canada
For enquiries visit www.barebackpress.com
For information contact barebackpress@gmail.com
Cover layout by Choi Yunnam

POEMS

Dedicated to the coaches of youth: "Peetoo" DuBoise, Willard "Beaver" Bard, David "Deisel" Decensi, Mike "Turk" Burke, and "Ripper" Gains.

DIFLUCAN

Wayne F. Burke

1.

"I is another."
Rimbaud

Happy Birthday

I get woke this morning
by a loud bang
sounds like a frag grenade;
I get up
on the wrong side of bed,
it is my birthday
(hooray)
at Rite-Aid where
I go to get my meds
I tell a clerk to go and
soak her head
after she calls me "Sir"
one too many times;
on the way out
some punk
bumps me
and I give him an elbow shot
and he say's "what the fuck?"
and I say's "what the fuck what?"
and he shuts-up
lucky for him
I am ready to rip his head off,
I don't know what possesses me;
I go into the bagel shop
which smells like burnt-something
and order from a slant-eyed Asian girl
who takes
like
half an hour to serve me—
I am getting pissed—
I see two cops at a table
and I say's to the girl
"smells like pork in here"
but she does not respond
maybe does not hear
one of the cop's stares
and I say's "what you looking at, Porky?"
and he say's "what did you say?"

and I say's "you heard me, I don't stutter."
"You got a problem?" he asks.
"Yeah—you."
They get up, walk over
the bigger of the two say's "let's go outside."
He looks just like my 1st sergeant
in the Nam
(a gung-ho mother)
"what? You think I am stupid?" I say's,
and he grabs me, or
I grab him,
I don't know which--
things go haywire quick
everything suddenly loud
and fast
too fast for me to catch-up with;
I cut-out,
a blackout
a total blank
and
do not come-to again
until in a cell
I wake with my face
in a puddle
of my sticky dried blood…
"Happy 65th!" I say's to myself.

Max

I got a room in the YWCA
which was immeasurably better than
sleeping outside
on a bench in the park though
the Y was not without problems,
like the roaches who
came out at night
and ran across my face
I tried to sleep with my mouth closed
but woke one night
after a tickling in my throat
and swallowed a roach
who started to walk around
inside of me
I could feel it
and would punch myself in the belly
and people probably thought I was funny
but I never could kill it and
finally
I went to see a doctor
and was given some pills
I took
but stopped after
over-hearing some trees talking
about me
I drank some Clorox
to kill the roach
but only made myself ill
and I went to the hospital
and had my stomach pumped
(I hate that)
and still the roach
I could feel it kicking
and getting bigger
and I decided to cut it out,
and bought a knife
for twenty dollars
but

before I cut
the thing came out
suddenly,
a healthy seven-pound boy
with little roach-face
and two adorably cute antennae.

Rusty

I thought I was hearing some Indian guy
chanting
saying his prayers,
the way they do
Oom...oom...
Kind of a murmur
louder and louder
until I woke
thinking wtf?
And got up
out of bed
and went to the window
and down below
about fifty yards or so
an orange truck,
and some guy
running a chain saw—
what the Christ!
I stuck my head out the window
and screamed
HEY!
And they looked up
one jerk waved
and they kept it up
tossing branches into the bed of the truck
and I shouted HEY!
But they did not even look,
ignored me
like I was not there
like I did not exist
like maybe I was a piece of shit
or something
and, I tell you
I was pissed—
had not slept more than two hours
or something like that
all night
and what gave them the right

I ask you
to wake people
at 6 AM
and break the city ordinance besides?
How rude and obnoxious
I stuck the barrel of my rifle
a 30.06
out the window
and
just to scare them
fired a shot over their heads
only
FUCK
I missed
and shot the guy in the side of the head
and he dropped
and I thought, hell
no use in stopping now
and I shot the guy who
went to the first guy's side
and then I shot the girl
standing by the truck's gate
(another head shot)
and the other guy
who had dropped the chain saw and
hid behind the truck
I could not get a bead on him
and put a few rounds into the engine block
to try and flush him
but he stayed put
until
as I reloaded
he made a run for it
and
in the old days
I would have got him
but I was rusty, see
and led the fucker a cunt-hair too much
the lucky prick
and, yeah

you might say that
I over-reacted a little
and maybe even that
I was wrong
but who are you to say anything
to me?
You wake me at
6 AM
on a morning after I have not slept
and before I have had my coffee
and see what you get
you son-of-a-bitch.

2.

cruel fate indifferent
as the gas company
to suffering humanity
wants the price
to be paid,
the bottom line filled-in;
the gods will not intervene
because
they too are waiting
for their piece of meat.

Raccoon

Pee Wee football practice over
and
I waited
under the streetlight
at the entrance to the field
for Gramp to come
pick me up
but he did not
and it got dark
then darker
the black silent night
the mountain in front of me
the purple sky
I climbed high up into a roadside tree
and watched a car
its red and yellow lights
go past
and stop
down the street
and I heard the car doors shut
and a voice
"look, it is a raccoon!"
And a rock
came out of the shadows
and flew past my head
and then I heard the door of the house shut
as the people went inside
and I climbed down
and stood
at the roadside
my useless helmet in my hand
waiting
until Gramp arrived,
a sheepish smile on his face
a mumbled apology.

Bat Man

No one wanted to be a dirty Jap
or Kraut
except Dickie Heller
who wanted to be
Kraut
because he was German
and his uncle had been in the S.S.
Dickie had a German Luger replica
and helmet he kept on his desk
in his bedroom,
the rest of us
were Americans,
Army, Navy, Marines, Green Beret,
we fought it out in the woods and
died ten times a night
but always came alive
for the next fight,
only Stevie Heney
never died,
not even after shot
point-blank
"you missed," he would say
and dance away
or
"I shot you first!"
He pissed us off
and some started to plot
his real demise or
something like it
and he must have got word
because he stopped coming
around,
stayed home at night
and watched Bat Man
on TV.

The Ruler

I sat in the first row
the last seat
too far back for Miss Good
the blind old bat
to see;
I did as I pleased,
ignored the lessons
and the voice up front,
one day
I looked up
from my story book
Miss Good stood beside me
her wattle-throat
and triple chins
red lipstick mouth
like a bow
thick glasses with gold rims
GIVE ME YOUR HAND, she said
and I passed it up
to her plump soft flesh
a ruler came out from
under her dress
she whacked my knuckles
like pounding in a nail;
my broken hand
I cried and
felt ashamed for
doing so,
no one even turned around to look
at me
the pain
the loneliness
she came back again
later
to hug and smooch
say how sorry he was for
beating me—
it was her schtick

she had no children of her own
we were it
hers to punish and then to kiss:
I did not hug back
because
the ones who did
got the ruler more often,
they were more satisfying
to her,
the psycho 3rd grade
Teacher of the Year.

Gold

My Uncle tells me to go
upstairs
run!
Bring back his bowling shirt
white with gold letters
yes master
right away
but I hesitate
and feel the pinch of his fingers
like pliers on
my earlobe
and am led around the
kitchen table
a kind of dance
not a waltz
a tango
of pain
that does not go
away when he
let's go
I carry it with me
up the stairs
and back down
through the years
the gold of the shirt
staining my hands
and nothing I could or
can do
to get the stain out.

R.I.P

Coach Gains, aka "Ripper," bear-like and
with a beer gut and mashed-face
stands in the center of the circle,
the woods around the field dark,
the mountain behind him
shaped like the Liberty Bell—
we sit on the soft grass
football helmets in our laps;
Coach Gains' gruff sepulchral voice
clear as a bell as he tells the
story of the "dirty player," a guy
whom Coach had played against
in Semi-pro ball; a guy who kicked and
punched and even bit in the pile-ups';
a guy "Ripper" vowed to get, and did
driving his helmet into the guy's gut
once, twice, three times, like a pile-driver
until the guy collapsed and had to be
carried off the field then taken to the
hospital where...he died.
"Let this be a lesson to you boys: play hard
but play clean! No dirty stuff!"
Cigarettes of coaches and fathers glowed
like fire flies; stars shone, and somewhere
six feet under, lay the dirty player, killed by
Ripper, who, during the day, drove a truck
for the Highway Department.

Sweat & Leather

Mr. Goldberg with a cigar in his mouth
and a line of tattooed numbers on
his arm
clomp-clomped in his boots
through the new shoe smell
with a box
full of tissue paper
and two shoes
for me
to try on;
I walked back and forth
over the carpet
as my grandmother watched
with a frown
eyeing the price tag
on the box:
"I want these," I said as
Mr. Goldberg chomped on his cigar.
Grandma flung the price tag from her
as if hot
and she sent Mr. Goldberg for
another box from
the dark corridor where grew the
shoes of
sweat & leather.

Penance

the retard-class at Howling Avenue Grammar,
taught by Charlie Baguette's father,
sold tickets each year to
support their activities;
Charlie and I found a box of them
in his father's study
and we took them door to door
in the neighborhood
selling each for a dollar.
We rode our bicycles up-street
to the toy store and
spent the money;
my grandmother asked me how I got the
new toys
and I lied
and she gave me dirty looks
all day and
the next
but I stuck to my fib
until Saturday
when I went to confession
and told the priest what
I had done
and he said
as penance
I was to bring the toys back
then return the money to the
people who bought tickets...
I thought of Mrs. Hellman
her hesitation and
flicker of distrust on her face
as she handed over the dollar,
and I knew I could not,
would not,
go back to her
or to the others.

Math

Mrs. LaBoy met with my grandparents on
Parent-Teacher Night
and afterward
they came home
frowning
faces nearly ashen
and Gramp had me get my math book and
sit down
at the kitchen table
where
he said
I would stay all night, or
maybe for
the rest of my life;
he showed me how to solve a few problems
and then he left
to go to work and
I got my story book out
HOW THE WEST WAS WON
and soon
I was on the trail with
Kit Carson
so deep in the Rocky Mountains
I did not hear Gramp
sneak in through the front door
I only felt the slap (feel it still)
to the back of my head:
I stuck with math
afterward
but never got the hang of it,
never did really trust Gramp again
either.

Wardrobe

I wore sneakers while growing up,
shoes were only for church
and had to last
no one was eager to put up 20 bucks
for new shoes
or for anything else;
I got two pair of new pants at the
start of each school year;
one I wore two days in a row
the other three days
and reversed the order the
following week;
one day while
waiting on the steps of the grocery store
for the school bus to show,
Mahoney the wise-guy glue-sniffing thief
said to me: "at least I have more than two pair of
pants,"
and I said, "well, we can't all have a wardrobe like yours,
Mahoney," which
got a big laugh and
caused Mahoney to
hate my guts more
than he already
had.

Ice Cream

A maple walnut ice cream cone
10-cents
at Eileen's Dairy bar
where Judy
a teenage waitress
Eileen's daughter
tall and slender,
"a rose yet to bloom"
I told Johnny Garibaldi
who had asked what I thought
of her
the words coming unbidden from
my lips
he blabbed it
and I regretted many times over
a rose yet to bloom
shouted on the street
on the school bus
I stayed away from Eileen's
until desperate for an ice cream
pistachio, butter pecan, black raspberry
I put my thin dime
into Judy's hand
and she did not say
anything except
"thank you."

3.

bent farmer-girl
plants thoughts
inside my head

Bathroom

I told the girl
sitting beside me on
the bus
that I had to use the bathroom
and as I stood
I heard her say "no thanks"
which
I thought odd,
and as I leaned against the bathroom wall
and pissed down the metal hole
while the bus swayed back & forth
I realized that she had thought
I had asked her to come with me
to the toilet,
something I had not considered,
ever,
even though I had been feeling her
tits since Denver…
Who or what did she think I was?
Not much, I guessed.
I got off the bus at the station in Rawlins
without asking her name
or number.

Debbie

dumped me without
warning or
any sign that
I could read;
a handsome girl with long hair,
large breasts,
I went to her room
and banged on her door
but she would not open;
I wrote a note but
she did not answer.
I felt as if I were being tortured.
I waited outside of her building
and when she exited
asked her what was going on,
and she became flustered,
started to cry,
and said she was sorry,
and so was I—
so sorry
for myself
I bought a big bag of
pot
and sat
in the window of my room
and stared below into a courtyard
and smoked
until
a week later
the bag
was empty.

Flute-o-phone

My grandfather wanted all his children to play
a musical instrument,
my father played saxophone,
I choose clarinet
squeak
squawk
I played the scale to applause
of the relatives
one Christmas Eve
it was the high point
as far up as I got
I quit practicing and
lost interest
though Gramp still bugged me
I wanted to go outside
play baseball
run around
the clarinet stayed in its velure-lined case
I took music-appreciation in Junior High School
but treated it as a joke:
In 9th grade I learned to play the skin-flute and
practiced daily.

Herb Tea

I met her at the dance,
a small shapely blonde
who told me she was celebrating
an anniversary
she asked me back to her a.p.t.
for some herb tea
and I followed
to her place
she gave me a tour
ending in the bed room
I said "very nice"
and she stormed away
into the kitchen and
started yakking on a telephone
and I waited for her
to finish
but she went on an on
like she had forgotten me
so
I waved and
mouthed "good night"
but she did not respond
only stared
and I left
without having had any tea
either.

#2 Pencil

I told the woman at the
art store
that I wanted the same brand of pencil
and paper that
Andrew Wyeth used
and she said, "Andy used a #2 pencil" and
as she moved around me
to the pencil case
her rear end brushed against me
and tip of my dick
and as she told me about the pencil
she looked at my cock and
I looked at her tits
and when she leaned to finger
some pads
my dick was plastered against her face.
"This is what Andy used," she said and
handed me a pad.
"What would Andy do in my situation?" I asked
myself.
"I will take it," I said,
and she stood, went
behind the counter,
and rang up the sale.
I put the #2 pencil in my pocket
and left.

Eclipse

When I was in the fourth grade
there was an eclipse of the sun
that Charlie Baguette and I agreed
to watch
using his father's telescope
and taking turns holding a green welding glass
up before the lens.
On the day of the eclipse I walked across the
backyards and the hot grass smelling
like broiled vegetation
to Charlie's house and
knocked on the door.
Charlie's mother stood in the screen window
squinting at me
one eye closed.
She wore a pink negligee:
"is Charlie home?"
"No, he is not."
Her tits spilled out of the
pink cups.
"Can I have a drink of water?"
 She opened the door only wide enough for
me to squeeze through.
The house smelled like sweat.
She turned and stepped to the sink.
I shoved my hand up between her legs and
she said, "Hey!"
I reached and grabbed the nipple of the
nearest breast.
She spun around:
I thought I would be slapped
but
she grabbed my head and
pulled me to her chest.
I sucked on the nipple and
jammed my hand down the
front of her
bikini pants

and started to finger
her snatch.
She moaned and her eyes
went blank
like stars,
no one home.
"Oh my god," she said
and slowly sank to her knees.
She pulled my wiener out of
my shorts:
It looked like an uncooked Jimmy Dean
sausage and
she snapped it up like a fish
taking a bait...
I heard Charlie enter:
"Ma!" he shouted, "what are you doing?"
"Mind your own business," she said,
"go to your room!"
Charlie turned and walked off
in a huff.
I forgot all about the total eclipse.

4.

"the stabbed man knows the steel"
Herman Melville

Streetlights

We used to stand in front of the
library
on Friday and Saturday nights
wearing our football jackets
red & white
lightning bolts down the sleeves
like stripes;
we said, "I shit you not" and
hocked gobs of
pearly spit
onto the sidewalk;
we said—whenever asked if
we had a date—"my name is in the
phone book."
We watched cars go past,
some with a guy and
girl inside,
and we imagined where
they were going
but not why
and we spat
and watched the streetlights come on,
watched the stars come out;
we said, "let's do something!"
Said, "like what?"
We never went into the library
except to take a piss
or else
follow some girl inside.

Linebacker

We walked in the woods on
a moon-lit night
a grove of trees
leaves crunching underfoot;
a bunch of us
guys
and one girl
and Starsky, a curly-haired runt
his face upturned
worm lips moving:
"go get her," he said
and gave me a shove—
she had long blonde hair
silver in the light
and walked by herself
upright
like the trees;
"get her!" Starsky commanded.
"Do it! You're a linebacker!"
She walked closer then
past
and as if not even seeing us.
Starsky poked me again,
the little prick;
he died that summer
in a car
that crashed and flipped onto
railroad tracks.
I was in the pool room
the morning after
when Fat Molloy came in and
announced,
almost gleefully,
"Starsky's dead!"

Schlump

I dove and stabbed the ball in the web
of the mitt
then threw
to the pitcher
covering the base
but
a second too late,
the game was like that
a dollar short
a day better spent
in bed
the 3rd baseman snow-coned a liner
I ripped,
the center-fielder caught my drive to the wall
over his shoulder
I could not buy a hit
all season
the bat went through the ball
like a magic trick
and the coach
a prancing chemistry teacher
knew less baseball than
I did the Periodic Chart
I disliked his face
his phony camaraderie
he did not earn
his place
I hit .146
--I think
maybe
I needed glasses
or
just more
luck.

Puke

One summer we drove 2000 miles
me and two others
in a Volkswagen Beetle
to find and pick psilocybin mushrooms
which we found in a pasture
on a back road
in Florida
led there by
a guy we'd met in a bar
who took us to his trailer
and brewed up some mushroom-tea
we each drank a glass of
before we three headed back
to the rest area we stayed at
and on the way
the guy in back puked
into an empty Styrofoam cooler
then asked, "what do I do now?"
and I turned to look at him
and he looked at me
and he lifted the cooler and drank
and when he was done
he said, "don't ever tell anyone," and
I said, "I won't," and
never did
until now.

Twenty

He comes up to me in the park
a kid in his twenties and
tells me his car is out of gas,
he is stranded,
has a pregnant girlfriend waiting;
he will pay me back double if
I lend him something
ha ha,
I am laughing at his style
"pretty good story" I say
"it is not a story."
I ask where his car is
and he answers
I ask what make of car
and he replies
I ask how he is going to get the
gas to the car
and he says he has a can...
I reach for my wallet,
peek inside;
just my luck to have only twenties,
I hand him one and
watch him walk off.
I kiss that sawbuck goodbye.

Book

My sister, the nurse
was a legend on
the maternity ward
she loved to work
spent the holidays
at the hospital
we never got along
growing up together
she stayed in her room
at home
only late in her life
did we talk
in emails back & forth
she bought and read each
of my published books
and then
she died
and in my dream
came back to sit beside me
on a couch
snuggled close
and read to me
from a book she held—
something that she never did
in "real" life.

The Shadow

Where the shadow ends
ahead
on the road
a crow flies, black,
gray, and white
as I make the bend
and two deer
mother and fawn
soft green and brown coats
dash into the woods—
if I had hit them
how bad
would I have felt?
I remember the chickadee
I killed
with a borrowed pellet gun
in the woods
I was young
a swarm of birds flew round and
round a tree trunk
in the green and yellow sun-splotched leaves
I shot into them
and one fell
at my feet
the other chickadee's stopped chirping
and disappeared
and oh
how sorry
I felt for the birds
whose fun I had ruined,
and for the dead one,
and for me
too.

5.

ice sheets on the river
the story of Winter
written on them

row of sharks' teeth
on the eaves—
bite of the cold wind

Shopping

I went shopping at Price Chopper
and walked around pushing a cart
up and down the aisles and
trying to remember what it was
that I needed to buy
and finally
I came to check-out
and pulled in behind a baby
in a bassinet
and I said, "hi baby," and
pulled on the baby's toe
and he moved his little foot
but not much
(had a pacifier in his mouth)
the mother, a blonde
had a harried-look to her pinched face
and three other kids jumping around her
and her cart;
the teenage girl cashier pleasantly curt
the bagger something of a dim bulb;
I left with my bags
under my arms
and without having connected to
anyone
in that place.

Larry

My friend Larry's obituary was not in any
major newspaper;
he was a little man
anonymous
a home-town creation,
part-owner of a granite shed who
one night
pulled another man out of
his, Larry's, ex-wife's bed
and when a cop
arrived
Larry picked up a shot gun
and pointed it at the cop
who pointed his pistol
in response
and in the stand-off
Larry said, "if you shoot me, I will shoot you,"
and Larry's relatives
who had gathered
shouted at the cop:
"shoot him! shoot him!"
but the cop, a rookie
was shaking too much to shoot
straight
and nobody died that
night
and Larry got off with probation
plus
six months to serve instead of
the years he could have got
and maybe deserved
for aiming a gun
at a cop.

Blarney

I went to J C Penny's to buy
a swim suit but
they had nothing remotely resembling
a swim suit, and
I bought a towel instead
and t-shirt with a pocket
(got to have the pocket)
and went home
and took a shower
and was excited to use the
new towel
which was soft and
felt good on my skin,
then I put my new t-shirt on
and walked downtown,
feeling good,
almost like a new man,
and I went to the meeting
but
it was not much,
same old members
same old blarney
stone shit
I thought
man
I have got to get me
some kind of
new life.

6.

at the dinner table my sister
threatens suicide—
pot roast again

walking into the nursing home to work 2nd shift
last rays of the sun
on my face

Henry Charles

Bukowski sits on a stool
at the supermarket cash register
fat-rolls around his belly and straggly hair
he wears a fire engine red supermarket shirt
and is bullshitting with a woman customer
instead of ringing me up
and I get upset
grab the glass jar of oil, or honey, or
whatever,
and stalk off without paying
and go to the back of the store
(I work there too, wear the same red shirt)
and meet Jigs, a childhood pal of mine
and say "fucking Bukowski is on the register"
and he says, "Chinaski?"
"Yeah."
We get onto an elevator.
The oil, or honey, or
whatever, is all over my fingers
because the jar leaks.

Geek

I moved up in the right-hand lane
to pass a big truck
on my left
but the truck sped forward and
I floored the Cadillac to get
in front,
before the two lanes became one—
and I moved to the left
and stopped at the light
and the truck squealed to a halt
beside me;
the driver barked down through
the open sun roof:
"YOU FAT BASTARD!"
"Fuck…You," I said.
"Say that to my face!"
I looked up:
"get fucked!"
He swore a blue streak,
the words raining down on me,
the truck engine growling;
I reached into my pocket:
"I will call the cops!"
(An empty threat as
I did not own a cell phone)
I watched him get out of the cab,
jump down,
a big muscled-up geek,
nickname of "Moose."
The light blinked green and
I made the turn,
glad we had not come to blows
though
that "fat bastard"
hurt.

Slip

It was Veteran's Day and
although I am not a vet
(my father was)
I decided to celebrate with a drink
or two
even though
I was on probation and
not supposed to drink alcohol.
I went out to a bar where
I got drunk and
became insulting,
asking a guy if he was with his girl
or his dog;
calling a waitress "dumb bunny";
interrupting a conversation between two girls,
and when ignored,
telling them to go and "finger each other,"
which got me thrown-out
but I was not done
and on my way out
grabbed a guy by the collar and
yanked him off his stool and
then found myself in the middle of a pile-up
of people
I had to fight my way through
to the door
and out
onto the sidewalk
where a siren I'd already heard
grew louder
and I started to run
like a son of a bitch
down an alleyway
and ran off the top of
a stonewall
and dropped
into the river
cold as ice

and the shock
I swam to the bridge
and hid in the shadow
I started to climb out
up the stonewall
but lost my grip
and fell back
into the drink
and got scared
I had to get out of there
or freeze
I started to climb again
my numb hands
the cold rock
almost to the top
the hands would not hold
the wall collapsed
I landed back in the icy stew
and started to yell "help!
help me!" and
lights in an apartment building
over the river
someone shouted from a window
a man and woman
showed up with
a rope
they threw down and
hauled me up
the woman asked if
she could help
and I asked if she would go out
with me
and she said "no"
and I walked away
over the snow-covered sidewalk and
toward my room
in a rooming house,
my shoes squishing with each step.

Shiva

I used to work for Mr. Goutay
from India
who owned a motel
he said "to-day we do a leetle plum-bing,"
connecting water pipes
and soldering them
something I knew nothing about
and I scorched my fingers on the blow torch
all because he was cheap and
refused to hire a plumber;
he drove a shitty used Volvo and
would drive ten miles out of his way
to buy a sandwich on sale
he licked the mustard packet
after he was done with it
and every now and then
he touched a fingertip to his forehead
and said, "see-wha!"
(the name of his god,
he told me).
After the plum-bing fiasco
he said that he could not pay me
and we argued in his car
until I thought about splitting his
frail-looking bald head, and
afterward, I did not work for him again
but every once in awhile
I would touch my forehead
and say "see-wha!"
but
I did not see that
it ever did me any good.

7.

early morning and the
gulf yawning
outside the hotel window

A Better Place

No corpse
just a box
with her ashes
in it
and her picture on the wall;
she went up in flames
to wherever—
a dark-eyed over-sized priest
who looks as if he stepped from
"The Godfather" movie
says that she is in Heaven
with Christ;
my older brother gives a eulogy
that makes people laugh and weep;
there is nothing else for anyone
to say
except for the priest
who insists that she is in
a better place,
to which
no one disagrees;
we put our coats on
and shuffle out the door
for the eats
at a restaurant which
none of us has been to
since the last funeral.

Suspect

I returned to the apartment
at midnight
after the last shift of
my work week
and got out
of the car
my sore legs and feet
the little Shih-Tzu dog
in the next apartment
began to bark at me
from an upstairs window
and I bent, picked-up
a rock and
threw it
and heard the window glass
break
and shards fall
with a sound like chimes
and a light came on
and I ran
around the house
climbed the stairs to my place
and sat
in the dark
listening to excited voices
next door
and watching for cops,
who never came,
and I went to bed
but before I fell asleep
that goddamn dog
started to bark
again.

Radio

He arrives in the pocket park
off Main Street
carrying a radio
and says to me
"I will shut this off in a minute"
and I nod and say "alright"
and I return to the drawing I am making
in my notebook.
"Hey! You!" he says
and I look up:
he has gray hair and a black patch over one
eye.
"I will shut this off in a minute."
"Fuck you."
"Oh, that's nice. I am trying to be a nice guy
and I run into a grumpy old man."
"Go somewhere else and be nice."
"I live here. Where do you live?"
"Get fucked."
"And the horse you rode in on."
He sits—
a vague presence in the corner of my eye.
I continue drawing until I am done.
When I leave will he say
"have a nice day?"
And if he does,
will I go berserk?
I hear him shuffle away but
he is back in half a tick
and sits
and sticks his nose into a book
and I get up
and leave
and am glad
I do not hear his voice
but wonder too
if I really do look old.

Colon: Not a City in Panama

I feel the thing go into and up
my ass
and it feels strange
plus
I feel as if I am about to blow
a big BM
all over the doc
behind me
but
it does not happen
because
they are suctioning me
as they run the tube up
and I am watching the
whole thing
on a screen:
a movie of my colon
pink, wet, and red-veined
segmented like a vacuum cleaner hose;
cramps begin each time the thing
rounds a turn;
a nurse presses on my abdomen
and after the initial panic
over the pain
I relax
the cramps do not last long
and I take-in the movie,
like a National Geographic special,
until a polyp appears
fat villainous jelly drop
the doc cuts off
with silver shears
in a gush of blood like
in a slasher film
but I feel no pain
just some unease that
the camera will show
another polyp

(and another, another, another)
but does not
and the doc says "that is it"
and
back in the recovery room the
nurse says, "you did really good,"
which
I take as compliment, thank you.

Acknowledgements:

I would like to thank the following publications, in which some of these poems have appeared: 13 Myna Birds, Commonline Journal, The Chiron Review, Your One Phone Call, In Between Hangovers, Ramingo's Porch, The Song Is, Horror Trash & Sleaze, Bold Monkey, Scarlet Leaf Review, haikuniverse, 50 Haiku, OPEN: Journal of Arts & Letters, The Rye Whiskey Review, Pangolin Review, Beatnik Cowboy, and Meat For tea.

About the Author:

Wayne F. Burke was born in 1954 to Claire Burke neé Kelly and Edward W. Burke. He was raised in the home of his paternal grandparents, as were his three siblings. His grandfather was owner and operator of BURKE'S INN, a generational business begun previous to the First World War. Wayne F. Burke attended public schools, and after High School, three institutions of higher learning before graduating from Goddard College in 1979 (B.A., RUP). After graduation he lived in a variety of places while working at a variety of occupations. In the mid-80's he located himself in the central Vermont area (USA) and has remained since. His first poetry collection (*Words That Burn*) was published when he was fifty-eight. Since then, three more collections have followed: *Dickhead*, *Knuckle Sandwiches*, and *A Lark Up The Nose Of Time*. A fifth volume, tentatively titled *Poems From The Planet Crouton*, is currently in progress.

Also by Wayne F. Burke

Words That Burn
$12.00
132 pages
6 x 9
ISBN-13: 978-0992035518
ISBN-10: 0992035511
BISAC: Poetry / General
BareBackPress

Praise for Words That Burn

"One of the most unapologetically honest books I have read...A poet who takes no prisoners, pulls no punches, wastes no words and knows how to tell a good story...Burke not only has the guts to admit his part in the fractured society he makes comment on, he also has the audacity to make art out of it...A sane voice in a mad world."

~ Matthew J. Hall,
Screaming With Brevity

"...the brutal evisceration of one man's experience of life on the planet earth. Burke writes with confidence, and swag...unforgettable imagery, black humor...something in these experiences that everyone can, or will, relate to."

~ Peter Jelen, author of
Impressions Of An Expatriate

"Burke is a tough young poet who, like all the rest of us, has learned some lessons from William Carlos Williams, but without imitating Williams. Burke writes the language of where he came from and with respect for it, and more power to him."

~ Alan Dugan,
Winner of *The National Book Award*
and the *Prix de Rome.*

Dickhead
$13.00
108 pages
5.25 x 8
ISBN-13: 978-1926449050
ISBN-10: 1926449053
BISAC: Poetry / General
BareBackPress

Praise for Dickhead

"These are wonderful, honest, hard-hitting poems. I loved every single one. NO ONE ELSE is writing poems like this, rooted in the real world, and with such a powerful voice."
~ Howard Frank Mosher,
*author of A Stranger in the Kingdom
and Walking to Gatlinburg*

"DICKHEAD is full of paradoxical twists, wordplay, subtle associations and darkly funny atmosphere. (Burke) is an earthy pragmatist with a surreal inner life...an insomniac dreamer."
~ Ada Fetters, Editor,
The Commonline Journal

"...a monster among us, a dangerous beast...reads like the best of Bukowski. Dead serious, no nonsense and it feels absolutely true. Burke swaggers through with such confidence you could almost resent his elan."
~ Michael Dennis,
Today's Book of Poetry

"DICKHEAD is about becoming a man, it's about the boy inside who still skips and sings, it's about the grind and coming to terms with self, it's about fantasy, reality, connection, ugliness and beauty; most importantly though, it is a book and a body of work that asks more questions than it answers. The word genius is bandied about far too freely, and most geniuses are not recognized as such in their life time. With that being said I am not the least bit hesitant in claiming Burke's poetic genius and I hope it is recognized in his lifetime."
~ Matthew J. Hall,
Screaming With Brevity

www.barebackpress.com

Printed in the USA
CPSIA information can be obtained
at www.ICGtesting.com
LVHW090920070124
768343LV00006B/191